Bibi Saves the Trees

by Judith A. Ewa

Published by Aya Press

Illustrated by Solomiia at GetYourBookIllustrations
Cover and Book Design by Kezia at GetYourBookIllustrations
www.getyourbookillustrations.com

Hardback ISBN-13: 979-8-9911577-3-5
Paperback ISBN-13: 979-8-9911577-4-2
eBook ISBN-13: 979-8-9911577-5-9

Ewa, Judith
Bibi Saves the Trees / Judith Ewa
Bursting with curiosity, a school outing to a forest reserve fills Bibi with respect for every life-giving tree. So her heart breaks upon discovering her family's favorite picnic spot has been cleared by saws and axes.

Inspired to restore the land, will Bibi's enthusiasm encourage her friends to take action?

Publisher's Cataloging-in-Publication Data

Names: Ewa, Judith A., author. | Solomiia, illustrator.

Title: Bibi saves the trees / Judith A. Ewa ; illustrated by Solomiia at GetYourBookIllustrations.

Description: Sheridan, WY : Aya Press, 2025.| Series: Preserve the planet ; 3. | Includes color illustrations. | Summary: Bursting with curiosity, a school outing to a forest reserve fills Bibi with respect for every life-giving tree. So her heart breaks upon discovering her family's favorite picnic spot has been cleared by saws and axes. Inspired to restore the land, will Bibi's enthusiasm encourage her friends to take action? | Audience: Ages 5-8.

Identifiers: ISBN 9798991157735 (hardback) | ISBN 9798991157742 (pbk.) | ISBN 9798991157759 (ebook)

Subjects: CYAC: Trees -- Fiction. | Forests and forestry -- Fiction. | Biological systems -- Fiction. | Environmentalism -- Fiction. | Community organization -- Fiction. | LCGFT: Picture books. | BISAC: JUVENILE FICTION / Science & Nature / Trees & Forests. | JUVENILE FICTION / Science & Nature / Environment. | JUVENILE FICTION / Social Themes / Values & Virtues.

Classification: LCC PZ7.1 E93.T74 2025 | DDC [E]--dc23

Printed in China

Dedication

To the unsung heroes who care for our Earth—
thank you for planting hope, one tree at a time,
and showing the world what quiet courage looks like when
it comes to preserving our planet.

And to every child who turns these pages—
may you always remember that even the smallest hands
can help grow a forest, protect the land
and shape a greener, kinder future.

The children held their breath as
the school bus crawled up the hill.

Leaves glowed in the warm shades of autumn. "Awesome view!" said Bibi.

Polly took deep breaths. "Smell the clean air!"

Nate sat with his eyes wide open. The class field trip to a forest reserve was off to a beautiful start.

The forest ranger waited as the school bus rumbled through the main gate and hissed to a stop. "Welcome," he said with a bright smile.

"Are you ready to learn about trees?"

Heads bobbed up and down as the class replied, "Yes!"
The deputies handed each child a flyer listing the names and pictures of trees in the forest reserve. After some basic safety instructions they started out on the main forest trail.

The forest ranger pointed out trees listed on the flyer. "Trees are an important source of food, medicine, shade and shelter for human beings, animals and insects," he explained. "Trees also improve the air quality through photosynthesis."

The class sat in a clearing surrounded by trees. A stream babbled close by. "The forest reserve is also an *ecosystem*," the forest ranger said. The children spotted lots of animals and insects, which they drew in their scrapbooks.

"Trees store water, and their roots help to hold the soil together to prevent erosion," he added. He warned about the dangers of cutting down too many trees, which could lead to *deforestation*.

Nate's hand shot up.
"Why is deforestation bad?" he asked.

"Deforestation causes a loss of shade, which can lead to high temperatures. High temperatures can cause harsh weather, such as droughts and floods. High water temperatures make underwater plants grow too fast, which means they reduce the amount of oxygen available in the water for fish to breathe," he replied.

How can I save the trees?

"Can we plant trees to replace the ones that were cut down?" said Bibi.

"Yes," he answered. "In fact, *reforestation* is the term used for replanting trees."

Bibi and her classmates thanked the forest ranger and his deputies and headed home.

That weekend, Bibi and her family went to their favourite picnic spot. When they arrived, they were speechless, unable to understand what they were seeing.

"Oh, no!" Bibi cried, her chin quivering. "They've cut down all the trees!"
There were no picnic tables, benches, playgrounds, or pathways lined with flowers. This area, which had once been green with plenty of trees, was now bare, dry and dull.

How can I save the trees?

The next day at school, Bibi told her teacher about her idea.
"I want our class to organise a tree-planting event. I have found the perfect spot,"
Bibi said with a twinkle in her eye.

Bibi assigned tasks to her classmates.

One group of children would contact the local garden centre for the tree seedlings.

Another group would make flyers and hand them out in town.

Their teacher got permission from the school's head and the local authorities.

On the day of the event, everybody showed up, including volunteers and the local TV station. The local garden centre had prepared the land a few weeks earlier.

They brought all the planting tools and the tree seedlings.
They showed everyone how to plant the seedlings.

Bibi organized her class and the volunteers into three groups. Row after row, one group planted the seedlings. Row after row, another group watered them. The third group spread mulch at the base of the seedlings.

After several hours, they finished planting.

Bibi, Polly and Nate looked out over the newly planted seedlings. "I can't wait to picnic here in a few years and see other families having a good time in the shade of our trees," Bibi said.

She imagined how wonderful it would be to see
the leaves glow in the warm shades of autumn.

Bibi thanked everyone for their hard work.

"Great job! We all worked together to save the trees!"

The End

Do you want to become an agent of change by promoting climate action? Tree planting is an ideal way to work with your community to protect the trees and the environment. Here's how:

How to Host a Tree-Planting Event Guide

Steps for Hosting a Tree-Planting Event

6+ Months Before the Event

- Select a site.
- Identify sponsors.
- Set up a planning committee.
- Analyse needs and costs.
- Set a budget.
- Raise funds.
- Set a date.

3 Months Before the Event

- Get permission and apply for permits.
- Select tree species and number of trees.
- Recruit volunteers.
- Prepare event programme.
- Order trees and supplies.
- Plan media campaign.

2-3 Weeks Before the Event

- Prepare the site.
- Launch media campaign.
- Send out invitations to local residents, elected officials, religious leaders and special guests.

Day Before the Event

- Tree delivery
- Supplies delivery

Day of the Event

- Assemble equipment and supplies.
- Set up registration desk for volunteers.
- Set up refreshment tables.
- Set up first-aid table.
- Welcome address.
- Instruct volunteers and demonstrate proper planting.
- Organise volunteers into 3 groups (plant, water, mulch)
- Take photos during the event.
- Closing remarks.
- Clean up site.

After the Event

- Media coverage of event (press release, social media).
- Water, weed, mulch and prune trees

Glossary

Deforestation:

The process of cutting down too many trees in a given area.

Ecosystem:

An area where trees, plants, insects and animals live together and depend on one another to survive.

Mulch:

Any material used to cover the surface of soil such as compost and bark chips. It serves as a natural weed barrier to reduce the amount of weeds that grow around a tree. It also helps to keep the soil's moisture in the ground and ensures that the roots of a tree or a plant are kept cool.

Photosynthesis:

A process by which trees absorb carbon dioxide from the atmosphere and release oxygen back into the air, making it safe to breathe.

Reforestation:

A process of replanting trees to replace those that have been cut down.

Author's Note

Visit my website: www.judithaewa.com to discover the other two books in the Preserve the Planet Series: *Bibi Saves the Honey Bees* and *Bibi Saves the Ocean*.

If you would like to support climate action in Africa, promoting initiatives that "heal, restore and protect landscapes", please make a donation to the Green Planet Initiative 2050 by visiting their website: https://www.gpi2050.org

Note for Parents or Educators

If you would like to receive a free *Bibi Saves the Trees* Activity Book, visit my website: www.judithaewa.com

Follow me on my social media platforms to share photos of your tree planting events:
Facebook: https://www.facebook.com/judithaewaauthor
Instagram: https://www.instagram.com/judithewa_author/
Email: judith@judithaewa.com

Leave a Review

If you enjoyed reading *Bibi Saves the Trees*, will you please consider leaving a review on Amazon, Goodreads or your platform of choice? Reviews help self-published authors find more readers like you.

About the Author

Judith A. Ewa is an award-winning children's author. Her latest children's picture book is *Bibi Saves the Trees*. Her international career as a finance professional, currently working in the area of climate change, has spanned the areas of humanitarian assistance, sustainable development and peacekeeping. The focus of her career has been on improving the lives of children around the world, especially in developing countries.

Her latest work is the third and final volume in the Preserve the Planet series. The first two books in the series include *Bibi Saves the Honey Bees* and *Bibi Saves the Ocean*. Through her books she aims to bring awareness to children about the importance of preserving the environment. Each book also offers a simple solution that children can actively carry out to bring about small changes today, to make a big difference tomorrow.

Judith holds an MBA from the University of Leicester. She enjoys listening to jazz, is an avid football and tennis fan who currently resides in Switzerland. Find out more about Judith at www.judithaewa.com

Printed in Dunstable, United Kingdom

73190777R00022